# Veins of Midnight

## The Mindscape of Obscurity

AASHNA KHANNA

*This has been my story for three years, and now it's all yours…*

# Contents

# Foreword

*In every couplet, a thought unfurls its chiaroscuro wings,*

*An unheard whisper of untold things.*

-Aashna Khanna

# Preface

"Veins of Midnight" is not merely a collection of poems; it is a testament to the raw and unvarnished thoughts that arise when the world's distractions lose their grip. It is then that we are most confronted with a tangled web of thoughts.

In this anthology, I have endeavoured to capture elusive moments and musings that come unbidden but carry substantial weight. Through writing, I was able to transform the weight of these experiences into meaningful expressions, which offered me some clarity.

Each poem is a fragment of my own journey, shaped by the shared experiences of life'strials, tribulations, and fleeting joys. These poems speak of the universal human condition, where one is both the architect and prisoner of his internalisations.

At its heart, "Veins of Midnight" grapples with the relentless dualities of existence- connection and isolation, hope and despair, clarity and confusion, truth and illusion.

Through these poems, I sought to illuminate shadowed counterparts of my mind, not with judgment or finality, but with curiosity and acceptance.

For where there is light, there is inevitably shadow.

# Acknowledgments

I want to thank all the people who have been a part of my journey—from family to acquaintances to strangers—for inspiring and shaping the experiences that have found their way into these pages.

# Prologue

*When the clock struck twelve...*

# Clock

In one corner, a clock hangs on a wall,

Its steady ticks echo through the hall.


Not just a tool to measure fleeting time,

But a keeper of stories, an unidentifiable paradigm.


Each tick, a heartbeat of moments gone by,

Each tock a reminder of the remainder till we die.


Its hands, constantly move in a perpetual round,

Tracing paths where memories are found.

The face it wears is marked with age,

A silent witness to rapture, remorse, and rage.


Its hands move forward, yet circle the same,

An endless ritual bound to its frame.


Yet in its silent yet rhythmic beat,

Lies a record, explicitly bittersweet.

It shows us the present, while we yearn for

the past,

For it is only nothingness that could last.


While the clock stands, both ancient and new,

It holds the truth we all pursue.


A needle that measures the time to

which we survive,

*It unlocks the present, locks the past, and*

*holds the future in guise.*

# A Teenager's Diary

Awake, yet weary in a ceaseless plight,

Exhausted in the morning, lost in the night.

Strung out and striving to grasp what's alive,

Through caffeine and validation, I'm trying to
survive.


Apathy's wrath feels so relentless,

It seems I'm teetering on the edge of 'senseless'.

The arrows all point, but none reveal the path,

As if leading me to falsehood is their

orchestrated craft.

Effortlessness with effort, let sleep's inebriation rule,

Each fading hour is a tiring but decadent fuel.

Names fade in obscurity's ceaseless din,

The things you've achieved have been a hollow win.


So, ink your skin with fleeting reverie,

You know there's a sinner deep within the sanctuary.

If the need arises, let the anguish be heard,

For people *hear*, but never *listen* to your word.

In this endless loop of ceaseless folly,

They tell us to see past the melancholy.

I'd rather seize the moment, revel in the excess,

Maintaining a good reputation is ephemeral,

instead-


Let the reputation fade, adorn yourself with transient
art,

The abyss is the only place a devil can play his part.

You pulled yourself into the cruel strife,

*In a world where death is the only guarantee of life.*

# Poison

It's funny how poison seems so slight,
A drop for death, yet daily doses while we survive.

In tiny drops, it steals life, a silent thief,
Promises escape yet bind us in belief.

We toast to the venom, glasses raised high,
Numb to the slow kill, as moments pass by.

Each sip is a paradox, both life and demise,
We choose our poison, behind weary eyes.

In daily doses, it lingers, unseen,

A bitter sweetness, toxicity in our routine.


It's the choices we make, the lies we swallow,

The fuller dreams we abandon, the empty we
follow.


We drink it in habits, in words left unsaid,

In the nights spent restless, engaged in battles in
our head.


Funny that it's not the fatal dose that kills,

But the daily drops, the silent ills.

A life of slow poisoning, we learn to endure,

Seeking virtues in vices, believing it's a cure.


Yet, in the end, we find, with a sobering dread,

That the poison we've cherished has left us half-
dead.


So, let's toast again to the bottle of poison, in
which we find,

*Life's true toxins lie in the mind.*

# Stardust

We lie on hallowed ground harrowed to its core,

The obelus appears to be brighter than before.

"Can you see that star?" you ask with hope,

If only tragedy wasn't our oeuvre's trope.


"I see it," I answer, though my heart knows,

It's shadowed counterpart is the region that glows.

"We can revive ourselves; we've come far."

Your voice is trembling beneath the star.


"Some stars," I whisper, "collapse fast,

*Their light becomes a shadowed memory that cannot last.*"

"But we haven't faded away" you say,

"*Stars need darkness to shine, not the light of the day.*"

I pause, and the silence hangs heavy in air,

*"That star you're pointing to isn't anywhere."*

I see the hurt, the refusal in your eyes,

Still clinging to truths that have transformed into lies.


"You can't give up," you say, staring at me,

"You had once thought we were meant to be."

"But love, my dear, it's fragile as light,

And we're chasing shadows long-lost to the night."*


"But we can reignite what we had and survive"

"What we had is something I would die to revive."

"You can't force the stars to realign,

When their fires have flickered and resigned."

"We followed each constellation, tracing its line,

Ignoring our slow and steady decline."

"You looked at the sky, seeing only the glow,

While I saw the darkness we've both come to know."


"We're still connected" your voice cracks again,

But connection means nothing when it's all pretend.

"Now, we stand on opposite ends of the same shore,

Watching the ripples of a love that exists no more."


"No battle remains," I say with a sigh,

"We're staring at stars that have already died."

"But can't you feel it? The fire's not gone"

Your voice is trembling as you carry on.

"I feel the warmth, my love, that still burns inside,"

"That illusion has burnt us." I quietly chide.

"Illusion? How could you say that to me?

"You might but, the stars don't disagree."


"They're remnants, my dear, don't you understand?

They died long ago in the palm of your hand."

*"I can't hold onto something that's already gone,*

Our love was a star, but even its light has moved
on."*


We sit in the stillness, worlds apart,

Feeling the fading beats of a dying

heart.

"What now?" you ask, your voice soft and resigned,

"Will we collapse like the star, and leave a void
behind?"

"We'll carry the memory, for that's all we can do,

But our future, my love, it isn't me and you."

"I thought we'd last forever, in love or in hate,"

"But even 'forever' must surrender to Fate."


I stand up slowly, your hand slips from mine,

We were living in a world where our stars didn't align.

"You'll find another sky," I say with a tear,

"And another star will soon appear."


I turn and walk, as the night grows cold,

Leaving behind a part of me that would grow old....

With you, as I walk away, you watch me depart,

But there's nothing more than *stardust* left in my heart.

# The Letter

"You think you need me, but you never did,

I was just a chapter you never tried to rid."


"Everything I gave you slipped right through

your hand,

The roses I planted now wilt on barren land."


"You say you loved me, but didn't leave a clue,

I paid the price; you never paid your due."


"I feel like I'd been living in lies,

I can't keep drowning in your alibis."

"You wanted me to fight, but you never tried,

You stood there waiting till it all died."


*"Maybe I was a lesson, one you never learned,*

*A book you borrowed, but never returned."*


"You'll never understand what you've done to me,

But I'll be gone, so you'll never see."


"Maybe one day, you'll regret this fight,

But I won't be here on your darkest night."

....

Yes, your letter arrived that day,

The words it carried cut away.


Your thoughts of me, my thoughts of you-

Were coming together as we both withdrew.


I opened its seal with a sharp knife,

Its words carved open the edges of my life.


But I didn't feel the pain as it cut through,

Because it only hurt as much as the thought of you.

*I couldn't smell the rose but I felt each thorn,*

Did you win me to lose me, and leave me forlorn?


I sealed my thoughts with the oozing ink,

I watched you sail away; you watched me sink.


Nights pass as I sit with my regret and tears,

Scribble through notebooks and waste the years.

*An ironic wrinkle in your life's design,*

*Because an ironed-out life was never mine.*


Your letter was written in blood but lined with rue,

It severed me, but not from you.


Yes, I got your letter, but I have nothing left to say,

The words spelled pain, and I'm sealing it away.

# Choice

In the course of life, we face a choice,

To heed the status quo or find our voice.

To tolerate the norm, and live up to its demand,

Or seize the reins with a determined hand.


For those who sit in silent resignation,

Surrendering to Fate without hesitation,

Will find themselves adrift in the flow,

*They have the boat but choose not to row.*

They say a drowning man will hold onto a straw,

Or drown in his thoughts and choose to withdraw.

He had always been hanging by the single thread,

Numbly holding on, alive when internally dead.


But those who don't simply choose to abide,

And dare to face the turbulent tide.

Of uncertainty mingled with a challenge ahead,

Don't dig the hole of their own deathbed.

So why stay bound to complacency's limit?
*When you could be the gun-holder,*
*why take the bullet?*


In our hands lies a choice that could
make or break,
Us, with the people around us at stake.

# He Stands on The Edge

He stands at the edge where the world seems to
pause,
Where the light meets the dark and the gain meets its
loss.
His smile is a dully plastered thing that gleams,
A blurred-out line of what is and what seems.

He breathes in the life, every scent, every sound,
In the hourglass of time, where each moment is
bound.
Each step that he takes is a step on a wire,
A brush against danger, a brush into the fire.

He's tasted the sweetness of life's finest wine,

And the intoxication of dullness beneath the luster

and shine.

Struggling in quicksand and sinking deep,

The unwanted things being the ones left to keep.


The world's spinning fast, but he holds it so still,

Timeless moments, but he bends them to his will.

The crowd doesn't see it, the mask that he wears,

The words underlying the ones he declares.


*Life is a masquerade, life is a play,*

*The edge of a breath, just a heartbeat*

*away.*

He stands at the brink, where life seems so long,

And so short, and so right, even when so wrong.

The ground that he walks on is firm and sure,
Yet its mortal sturdiness is something he can't
endure.
He's at the edge of it all, the end of the line,
But he laughs like a man yet to taste the divine.


The city hums beneath, oblivious to the fall,
Oblivious to his last breath, a sigh, and a release from
it all.
But the edge he's found isn't just in his mind,
It's where the ground gives away, and all is left
behind.


So he falls with a smile, the wind in his hair,
Not fleeing from life, but to something more rare.
In the final descent, he feels the most alive,
As he finds in the fall, his reason not to survive.

And the edge that once held him, both in life and
in height,
Is where he found his first and last flight.
*Not to end his journey, but for his soul to heal,*
*Which can only be done without the ability to feel.*


So he looks down below, sees the world far away,
He smiles yet again since he never had substance to
say.
*He's at the edge of life, but the edge of a building too,*
*And as he falls, he tastes the peace he never knew.*

# I Don't Want Any Other Shade but Blue

You don't know me, just my name,

And the rumours around it, ones I didn't claim.

My smoking gun, my wounded pride,

In plain sight but you think I hide.


My eclipsed sun, my darkened days,

A clear vision lost in a blurry haze.

This has broken me, torn me apart,

The target moved as I threw the

dart.


My twisted knife, your cruel deceit,

Seems like I progressed to see myself

retreat.

A sleepless night, a restless dream,

A suffocating silence that wants to

scream.

My fight in the dark, my endless war,

A battle I don't want to win anymore.

The world is a geoid, but mine has an edge,

I know because I've been standing at the ledge.


I haunt myself, the embodiment of a ghost,

I'm losing faith in the things I believed the

most. Hence, I don't want any other shade but

blue, Sadness is long-lasting, genuine, and true.


My best-laid plan, your cunning hand,

My hourglass stands with emptied sand.

My barren land, scorched by fire,

Has cracked open and into its own mire.

I don't see any other shade but blue,

And I've been living in the shades of this endless

hue.

For I forsook a part of me behind,

Now it lies shackled yet

unconfined.


Have you heard about the tragic end,

With scope to save but no use to mend?

You know, it hurt beneath these scars,

*Only in the darkness do you see the twinkle of stars.*

# Dark Love

His breath is a prayer, and I am the sin it names,

A confession that burns us but brands him in its

flames.

Each glance is a theft, a crime without shame,

And those flames bind me with a tether I can't

name.

His skin holds sins that we couldn't begin to

explain,

A map of unexplored treasures I want to claim.

His touch is a dagger that's explicitly mine,

But it doesn't cut back desire, making madness

divine.


I know this could ruin me and I should refrain,

But I am bound to him in pleasure and pain.


The curve of his dagger, the curve of his lips-

Is poison consumed in intoxicating sips.

His scent breathes a story of love and lust,

My chains of passion are ravaged but robust.


His touch is a cage that feels like escape,

And the freedom I crave while I'm wrapped

in his shape.

His gaze is a spell, a tempting trance,

A delicate waltz, now, a demonic dance.

...

The devils painted the town red, the brushes
unrestrained,

The tapestry of darkness was where their story was
framed.


Fate, a cruel puppeteer, pulled the strings,

A tragedy unfolded on flaming love's fragile wings.


Betrayal's bitter sting, a baleful kiss,

Their rich rose wilted, tumbling into the abyss.

Beauty lay in the darkness that seemed

lethal and dire,

*For sin was the altar, and they were the smoke of*

*its fire.*


*Every arrow shot by Cupid landed a miss,*

Each moment turned into one they'd reminisce.


And just when light started to descend,

*Their dark love became a story that began just to end.*

# Twisted Lullaby

In my cradle, I sat in a heap,

A twisted lullaby rocked me to sleep.


The night spilled ink, thick with dread,

And I drank it down, every word it bled.


The wind carved knives, left marks on my skin,

But I smiled through the sting, let the sensation sink
in.


Thunder kissed me, its lips rough and torn,

I begged for the strike, to feel wrecked and worn.

The rain fell like needles, a crucifixion laid,

*A demolished world indifferent to the effect of the grenade.*


Bruised by shadows, I bled in their shade,

And the deeper it cut, the more I stayed.


Pain swirled poison, intoxicating like wine,

I craved every drop, every hungover sign.


*I wore my wounds like jewels glistening with blood,*

I tucked away in my pocket a dying bud.


My frame throbbed to feel the tongue of the flame,

To yearn for the agony, my flesh was tame.

The blackened sky tore, but I laughed at its scars,
*For feelings were the compass that would lead me to the stars.*


Pain painted the world in shades only I could see,

The burden didn't feel burdensome when borne by me.


I bared my wrists to the rain's scathing bite,
Begged it to cut, to baptize, and blur my sight.


The cold is permanent after howling winds cool the
warm,
Everything shall cease to exist if the wrath is gone.

My flesh wore the bruises like petals in bloom,

My masochistic garden thrived in the drought and
gloom.


The storm raged, relentless, and I howled in its thrall,

For the darkness was mine, and I'd welcome it all.


Let the pain be my prayer, the blood be my creed,

In agony's arms, I find the embrace I need.


The rain kept falling, and I whispered for it to stay,For

the dark, stormy clouds were bright as day.

# This Man

He dons his suit, the fabric pressed and taut,

*He never liked ties, but that's something he forgot.*

The tie he knots is a ritual- it's precise,

*For this man, cash isn't the only price.*


*The mirror mocks with eyes that seem to see,*

*The weight of what society says he's yet to be.*

He buttons his shirt, pulls down the cuffs,

A man of few words, but his silence is rough.

The door swings wide, the world does await,

He steps into the office, but he is late.

The clock seems to tick louder through the day,

And when the working hours are over, and he is on his way-


He's told to work longer without question; to stay in line;

To burn himself out so that he doesn't fall behind.

Tired and taxed, but to four walls, he is confined.

*Lost in the hustle at the cost of his mind.*


His phone keeps ringing, a constant barrage,

His boss barges in to tell him who's in charge.

The emails accumulate, the tasks multiply,

But his 'manliness' should never begin to die.

At home, his children grow up too fast,

He smiles through the chaos, hoping it wouldn't last-

Just like everything else that he now missed,

Chaos too, should cease to exist.


His partner seeks a man who is there,

Who has more than his burdens to share-

Of deadlines and demands, of debts he must pay,

He's forced to break promises, but makes them everyday.


Because he wants to fulfil them, and one day he might,

When he becomes inconsistent in his plight.

His gaze asks for mercy; it's full of unnoticed plea,

But he's trapped in the world they refuse to see.

The tie is loosened, but still too tight,

As he faces another wasteful and sleepless night.

His neck aches, his shoulders tense,

But he's been given the gift of being a man; hence,


He smiles at the dinner table and chatters,

As his family and its security is what truly matters.

He moves like a vessel, his body a tow,

But his mind is darker than they'll ever know.


*The world demands strength to even his weaknesses,*

He's a man of one skin but he wishes for ecdysis.

The silence is deafening yet worth the keep,

Because if this man voices it out, he'll crumble in a heap.

Now he gazes at the mirror, tired eyes that reflect-

A man who gave all, yet has nothing left to protect.

And when the house falls silent, when all is still,

This man retreats into his mind, against his will.


The years slipped away, right from the palm of his hands,

His life had been spent in fulfilling demands.

*The suit is discarded, the tie untied,*

*But at his core, this man has already died.*

# On Her Darkest Night

On her darkest night, despair's cruel reign,

A knock resounded through the pouring rain.

She opened the door, full of contemplation and
dread,

To see a man she could've never imagined in her
head.


He stood there, smiling, with warmth in his hand,

But she shut the door; the encounter was
unplanned.

The warmth was something she'd never take,

Because in a matter of time, it would

fade away.


But he came again, on the very next night,

With gloom that chased away the choking

light.

She finally let him in when everyone else withdrew,

The more she gave, the more he chased someone
new.

Then one nostalgic night, he turned away,

No words could make his footsteps stay.

The door he had walked in through met its bitter
end,

As it slammed shut, fleeting moments time did
rend.


He took with him everything he gave,

Left obsidian voids in the space he'd paved,

Her heart, though, didn't bear the sting,

Of love's cruel theft, a heavy wing.


For in his wake, the night  returned,

And with it, all the pain she'd spurned.

The brightest flames, they say, must die,

Leaving nothing but tears to dry.

*A cruel twist, her victory brought more battles to fight,*

*Her world turned dark from blinding light.*

*He came, he healed, then walked away,*

*And gifted her wounds her love wouldn't let her repay.*

But again, her heart didn't bear the sting,
Because love is one peculiar thing.
That leaves its marks, which seem beautiful
despite the hurt,
She loved him till that door crumbled into the rainy
day's dirt.

# High School

Through high school, I was at the mouth of the gun,

*Every day a race, with no incentive to run.*

*It was not until a chapter beyond the text was turned,*

*That I pivoted through lessons learned and pages*

*burned.*


In corridors we've walked through for many a year,

Students still manage to hide their demeanour.

Danger and shadows loom overhead,

Each word needs to be thought-through and said.

A friend to me, is both, a friend and foe,

With more to hide and lesser to show.

Smiles are something we've all learnt to wear,

Fabricated into each blank stare.


Through high school's corridors, at the barrel's edge
I stood,
Overexplaining myself for I felt misunderstood.
I could never distinguish between the truths and the
lies,
*The threshold of beginnings and ends blurred before my eyes.*

It was not until betrayal's blade found its place in

my back,

That I realised I had no choice but to live upon the

wrack.

In the crucible of lessons and the ashes of bridges

scorched,

I unearthed the truth that the stele had torched.


Perfection's mirage is a distant shore,

Behind each laugh, there's something more.

Laughter resounds in the halls of youth,

Another fugitive glimpse of a hidden

truth.

Every year, constant changes unfurled,

Navigating the maze of a shifting world.

In quiet moments, we get to connect with our core,

Finding meaning that we'd failed to explore.


*Each misstep is a lesson in disguise,*

*The phoenix burns down to ashes,  but is destined to rise.*

The future is blighted, bleak yet bright,

A darkened picture of forthcoming

light.

# The Underdog

She was always seen by them all, but never known,

A presence in their midst, *surrounded by people, yet alone.*


She was always the underdog, hidden from their sight,

In shadows she remained though she could take the spotlight.


They watched her from afar, their glances swift and cold,

In their eyes she lingered, and in the rumours they told.


*In every crowd she tried fitting, wanting to fade away,*
*Because at least faded things mingled with decay.*

They clapped for her in jest; the applause that felt
thin,

For they saw just her image, not what lay concealed
within.


Her kindness was taken for granted, a gesture here
and there,

She wouldn't wrong anyone but get a prejudiced stare.


They knew her name and face, her limits, her
armored shell,

But the battles that she had fought were ones no one
could tell.


*She was either the misdirected boat or its misplaced oar,*

But her confidence started shattering like never
before.

Her efforts went unnoticed, her pain a blue bruise,

In a world of many choices, she was never the

one to choose.


In every race she ran, she squeezed her eyes shut
through the haze,

And their eyes skimmed over her, in all their fervent
gaze.


One day they'll realise she'd always been the

underdog,

One can't distinguish between the smoke and

the fog.


*She was seen by them, but never known at all,*

*The wounds they inflicted were scars only she could recall.*

And she'll use this to her advantage, an
unexpected attack,

And this time, she'll enter the battle to make it back.


For she'd always been defending, it was time to grab the
gun,

Survivors in the battle, apart from her, shall be none.


They had always mocked her when she was not in
their sight,

But she'd laugh at their faces; she'll do wrong for the
right.


As an anti-hero, but she'll be called the villain,

She would *help them* in mastering the art of submission.

But she won't be out for revenge; she'll be

out for justice,

To make her hit rock-bottom, they dug her a crevice.


But they never realised they were digging

their own grave.

They saved her the work, now it's them she

shall enslave.


They chose to be visible, she chose the shadows,

To be the underdog was an advantage only she
knows.

# Paradox

When she spoke, they questioned her thought,
When she stayed silent, they said she didn't speak a
lot.

In her solitude, they whispered of loneliness buried
deep,
In her interactions, they said it's not attention she
should seek.

When she dressed modestly, they labelled her as plain,
When she dressed boldly, they accused her of being
vain.

In her moments of calm, they called her detached,
In her moments of passion, they deemed her too
attached.

When she followed tradition, they criticized her
conformity,
When she broke norms, they scorned her for
deformity.

In her moments of strength, they saw her as cold-
hearted,
In her moments of vulnerability, they saw her as
thwarted.


When she chose the safe path, they questioned her
ambition,
When she took risks, they doubted her intuition.

In her success, they whispered of luck's lucky grace,
In her failure, they pointed fingers, quick to place.

When she sealed her lips, they accused her of fear,
When she uttered words, they said she should hear.

When she sought independence, they labelled her
proud,
When she sought help, they said she was using the
crowd.



In her moments of nothingness, they

questioned her resolve,
In her moments of action, they doubted her

ability to evolve.

In her moments of solitude, they accused her of

isolation,

In her moments of socializing, they questioned her
motivation.

When she spoke softly, they labelled her timid,
When she spoke boldly, they accused her of being
rigid.

In her moments of agreement, they saw her as
compliant,
In her moments of disagreement, they deemed her
defiant.

*When she took things earnestly, they called her intense,*
*When she laughed things off, they took advantage of her*
*innocence.*

But she knew that no matter what they said,
*Her worth wasn't defined by her image in their head.*

# Firefly

As the evening dimmed into the night,

I was a firefly, a beacon, with a tiny light.


In shadows where even darkness fears to tread,

I fluttered for you, lending Ariadne's thread.


Through whispers of the nocturne's breeze,

I sparkled, weaving warmth, and giving ease.


A tiny flame within the vast  unknown,

I gave you company, now I'm left alone.

As the night faded into the morning dew,

I faded after losing that neon hue.


Though fleeting like a dream in the midnight sky,

I was your firefly, lighting up your darkest sigh.


I wove dreams in the tapestry of your despair,

A flutter, I soared, creating a luminescent lair.


Lost in your shadows, I chased away the gloom,

Yet, as dawn approached, I faced impending doom.

For in lighting up your world, I dimmed my own,

A firefly's light got overthrown.


I was the beacon, guiding your forlorn quest,

Yet, in the aftermath, I found no place to rest.


In the world of shadows, I cast my glow,

I lit up the surface, got consumed in the undertow.


I illuminated your path with each delicate wing,

Yet, in the labyrinth of shadows, I lost my own string.

I lit up your world so that you could see,

And I don't know what became of me.


Thoughts, like my trails, linger in the dark,

Now I think of it as my flying lark.


I painted constellations with my ephemeral light,

Yet, in the void, I dissolved, consumed by the night.


Now, a fading ember, lost in the unknown,

I was your firefly, now in my light you roam.

# Love and Destruction

He traces my neck; I feel his cold breath,

A groan, a snare, and a promise of death.


I imagine our trysts, in whispers thin,

But without brushing a finger against his skin-


I couldn't have committed those impetuous sins,

When it's only in my head that it all begins.

I keep this unholiness suppressed and locked,

But for how long can longing be stopped?


I've been told no thought is inherently vile,

*Only deeds betray so, my sins remain in exile.*


In my mind, we've transgressed all those lines,

If it's mere illusion, I script the covert designs.


His gaze is a sin, a ruthless tide,

Of a burning sensation he cannot hide.

His touch reveals that love does maim,

If I'm losing my sense, I've lost the sense

of shame.


He follows like a shadow stitched to my skin,

Beauty is on the inside, should I let him in?


We've committed those crimes in my head,

He knows this although it remains unsaid.


So if I kneel, I'm both captive and queen,

In this throne of torment, where shadows convene.

Hands that punish, hands that pray,

*The devil himself, begging for me to stay.*


I loathe his touch; I crave his claim,

For he marks me with a force I can't name.


We built walls that we crashed right through,

Built from desire, now lined with rue.


He's branded his name into my mind,

I force myself to believe I'm not inclined.

The line is blurred between predator and prey,

He breaks me to shape me, while I shape him to stay.


And in his grasp, I find my demise-

A willing fall in those haunting eyes.


He watches me like a sin he's eager to taste,

Eyes a dagger, breath a brushstroke of waste.


His hands- violence wrapped in sweet deceit,

Ruin is the fate he makes me want to meet.

"Run," he murmurs, but I need him to seize,

And bind me till darkness becomes my disease.

I ache for the danger, the venomous thrill,

His touch a poison, his love a kill.

*I ignite the fire yet drown in his flame,*

Shivering each time he murmurs my name.

The unnamed way he holds me close,

Is the sacredness I crave the most.

These fatal fantasies have stolen my heart and breath,

Attaining him is disguised death.


He breaks me open, commits a beautiful crime,

And I fall willingly, every single time.


I navigate through a thorny maze,

He's worth the cuts in my fevered craze.


For love and destruction walk the same line,

And it is in his darkness that I choose to shine.

# Stones

I've hoarded stones as memories, seared in thought,

Uncertain if they're talismans or ruins time forgot.

Some dully glint with secrets only silence can spell,

Others weigh down like debts that I owe to myself.

Each stone is a memory, both nebulous and defined,

*But a treasure is only valuable when left behind.*

Are they relics to cherish, or burdens we've amassed?

A steel-grip on misgivings of shattered glass.

Each stone I've gathered is an indentation of the

past,

But will they stones forge us, or fracture at last?


*Will these fragments coalesce into an engagement ring,*

*Or shatter into splinters sharp enough to sting?*


We hold these pieces, coarse and unrefined,

Did each milestone we reach form a cage around

our mind?


*This path is paved with relics, in remembrance of our vow,*

*And I can't tell if it anchors or drowns us now.*

If I cast them into water, would the ring let

the weight dissipate,

Or pull me under the depths with every stone

I negate?


Each step is a question: Do we create or erode?

Or hasten the decomposition of our treasured

hoard?


So here they remain, in pockets, and in hand,

Knowing only their weight, to cherish or to
withstand.

# The Hunted Hunter

I'm the hunter that was once the prey,

I left a trail to be left astray.

Primed for combat, tamed to be wild,

I'm the executioner that needs to be exiled.


Struck, but never killed, I've paid my due,

Darkness was a companion I once knew.

Is truth just a vision, a reflection, a sign?

Or a reality that's merely our mind's design?

I've lost the quiver, now sharp arrows fly,

Words once abandoned, now pierce the sky.

Easy they come and painfully they go,

For the arrows are shot with a broken

bow.


From prey to predator, with less to hold,

And lesser to live for, battlements cold.

*Trying to stay grounded as I seek flight,*

*In a world that's ablaze, I search for darkness, not light.*


I've been the hunted, cowering low,

Now I'm the hunter, my prowess does grow.

Who could ever leave after the power they see?

But who could stay through this fierce legacy?

Searching the darkness, confronting each fear,

What if I find peace as the end feels near?

*Through gritted teeth, I meet each affliction,*

*Hoping answers might emerge from my own*

*contradiction.*


Pacing the night, as someone with resolve,

In flames of ambition, a spark could evolve.

Heroes may falter, from Hell, I rise anew,

I hold on by letting go of the heroism I knew.

From hunted to hunter, I no longer relent,

Guarding what's mine, earned through
what I've spent.

They see right through me, but I'm
unafraid,

For I was what they broke, and I am what
they've made.


The transformation will never tell you
when,

It occurs, but it couldn't fracture you again.

I've been the hunter, I've been the prey,

It was the very scent I chased that led me
astray.

# Calumny

Everyone in life has a reputation,

Sometimes seen with contempt, sometimes with
admiration.


It takes years to build, with care and toil,

Yet it crumbles fast, leading to turmoil.


A word, a glance, a rumour sown,

Can tear down walls that took years to hone.


You sacrifice several moments to build a name so
sound,
And a mere moment that can snatch it to the ground.


The irony is stark, the truth severe,

How swiftly trust can disappear.

But in the chaos, amidst the storm,

Pay attention to those who keep you warm.



And those who stoke the flame till all is lost,

The relationships you maintain and

how much they cost.



For in life's tumultuous  path,

The candle wavers to face pure wrath.



*When masks slip and illusions fade,*

*They reveal nothing but a masquerade.*



Fleeting glories, popularity and fame,

A flickering flame in a ruthless game.

For what is gained with deceit and lies,

Soon crumbles beneath truth's piercing eyes.


For reputation's a fragile thread,

Easily severed by words misread.


Calumny is one sweet sting,

That they see as the essence of everything.


So remember well the ones who stay,

When your reputation fades away.

# Taste Heaven in Hell

Become the devil that tastes the divine,

Seize the day for the darkness to shine.

Live like a devil, paint the town,

Thrive in the moments in a world upside down.


You're shackled to the world, a weighted chain,

Upon unshacklement, nothing shall remain.

The road is long, and it twists with dread,

So taste life before you're dead.

Grab the rope before your head is hung,

*Life is a race that can't be overrun.*


Break the broken, ignite the fire,

Descend into chaos to feed your desire.


Society can sneer, call you vile,

But they'll all crumble to dust in a while.

*Why bend according to society, simply bend the law,*

And savour each wicked thrill raw.


*If life's lifeless, it isn't worth the keep,*

You're alive with a pulse that has the right to seep.

Into the crashing wave of the forbidden,

Taste the sweet from the sin you're given.

In the end, we're all the same,

Bones and dust, all wrapped in one game.

Let them be your judge, let people hate,

They won't matter at Heaven's gate.


You're marching to the end, no matter the name,

You're a rotting corpse with a grave to claim.

*So before you get there, you must dwell,*

*In the paradox of Heaven- living Hell.*

# Purpose

## Him:

"Life is purposeless." one claimed with a sigh,

A search for meaning where none apply.


"We're chasing after the worthless, and believe in
Fate,

In a world that's a cold and indifferent blank slate."


Why chase a purpose when in the end,

We're dust, forgotten, as we blend


Into the void from which we came,

"Life's a purposeless cycle." was his claim.

Life could be a gift; living could be a disease.

But purpose is a crutch to calm unease.


Humans invented Gods and Fate,

To explain the void, to fill the blank slate.


Isn't it easier to say 'we're here for this,'

Than admit life's random- hit or miss?"

# Her:

"Random? Look at the start of new life, a newborn's
cry,

Is there no purpose when they first try.


To breathe, to grow, to learn, to be?

It is purpose that's their first step, you'll see."


"It's in the struggle of life that purpose is found,

But as the newborn grows, the ultimate goal fades
into the background.


Purpose isn't perfect, nor the journey kind,

But it's in the process, the search, the grind.

Without pain, would we seek to heal?

Without loss, could we learn to feel?


Life's not a script, but an ongoing play,

Where purpose is found in the roles

we portray."

# Him:

"But you ignore how the world truly spins,

Wars and suffering, chaos within.


Where's your purpose in a mother's tears,

Or the child who dies before their years?"


"Then it's not real! Just something we say,

To justify why we wake every day.


A comforting lie, to stave off despair,

That life has meaning, that someone cares."

# Her:

"It's not a lie, but a lens we choose,

Purpose is the path we refuse to lose.


Yes, the world has chaos, that I won't deny,

But even in darkness, purpose is seen by

the inner eye.


It's in our choices, in the paths we take,

In the connections we form, and the bonds we
make.


Purpose is handed down from above, but it gets lost
in the strife.

Tainted by forthcoming experiences in life.

# Him:

The other sighed, still unconvinced,

But in his heart, a question pinched.


"Is life even worth living?" he asked thinking of his
dreams,

Without purpose, nothing would be as it seems.


But when we choose to make our object real,

Purpose is the innate fire we feel."

One saw the world as cold, distant, and detached,

The other saw purpose, and a life unmatched.

Both opinions valid, both real, yet worlds apart,

Two perspectives, from the bottom of each heart.

# Haunt Me, Don't Love Me

"Haunt me," he whispered, " instead of love so brief,

Happiness is transient as compared to grief.

Dreams are forgotten with morning's light,

But nightmares linger through the day and night."


"Be my shadow, haunting and stark,

In every corner of my mind, every igniting spark.

Love's flame can wane, can flicker and die,

But your haunting presence, will forever lie."

"In love, hearts break, despite giving it our all,

But haunt me, and I'll resiliently face the final downfall.

Love is dependent, it may dim and cease,

*"Your nightmarish touch is my disease."*


"Love can weaken, can freeze or turn cold,

But your ghostly touch will never grow old.

Haunt me in memories, in whispers of air,

In the silence of rooms, where we once were there."

"Be the chill that engulfs me and my skin,

The unseen force, propelling me within.

*You don't remember dreams by morning, they wither away,*

*But a nightmare's nature itself is to stay.*


"Take over me," he said, "with every sigh,

Because it's these tears that never run dry. For

love may leave, and we may drift apart, But

your ghost, my love, will own my heart."

"Your presence keeps me away from a dream,

The sound that rings over and over is a scream.

Love is fleeting, a momentary kiss,

But if you haunt me, you'll be someone I could never miss.


"In the hourglass of time, in the depths of my mind,

You'll be someone I'll be forced to find.

For love is mortal, but haunting's divine,

*So haunt me, my love, and eternally be mine.*"

# Euphoria

Hesitation graces the tremulous breath,
A powdered trail of dopamine leading to death.
Uncertain sighs on a wavering path,
*Foreboding the pleasure in the silence of wrath.*


Euphoria unfurls in crystalline taste,
A rush of elation through time and space.
Alluring whispers that push us to thrive- in Hell,
The drug's sweet ring, the very knell.


A novice trapped in the recurring cycle of a scheme,
*The nightmare of a high, disguised as a dream.*
Nostalgia draped in the ecstasy's sheen,
Sufferance in a packet isn't hard to glean.

Dulcet murmurs of pleasure's renewed guise,
*Each inhale is of a veiled paradise.*
The euphoria hits the vulnerable mark,
Blinding light is as dangerous as encroaching dark.


Resigned to the pattern of repeated use of the vial,
A habit's cold, unfeeling clasp was merely a trial.
A lingering ache where once pleasure lay,
The fleeting euphoria has drifted away.


The intoxicant's promise dissolves in the air.
A disenchanted whisper ringing everywhere.
Dust settles in the drug's final toll,
A final surrender of the numbed-out soul.

# Sleepless Nights

In every resigned breath, a flicker dies,
The weight of unspoken truths in my eyes.


Each midnight tear that stains this page,
Reflects the buried chaos and silence of rage.


Every syllable is the sound of the years' pain,
*The drought ended with incessant rain.*


I chased meaning while I was in the dark,
I sought a silhouette in a future that was stark.

A fragile tome of perfect despair,
The ink's now smudged everywhere.


Through labyrinths of thought, I didn't calculate
the cost,
Of the oblivion in which everything I gained was
lost.


Each line is a bridge to worlds you'll never see,
My distant self closes in, consuming me.


The sleepless nights, a sea where dreams have
drowned,
*I am the sail and the very anchor pulling myself down.*

# Epilogue

*In every couplet, a thought unfurls its chiaroscuro wings,*

*A written whisper of unspoken things.*

# About the Author

At sixteen, Aashna Khanna presents "Veins of Midnight: The Mindscape of Obscurity," a compelling anthology that captures her journey as an adolescent.
An avid reader from an early age, she channels her literary passion into this collection, exploring the nuances of her experiences through insightful reflections and observations of both her life and those around her.

Beyond her role as an author, she designed both the front and back covers, imbuing the book with a distinctive personal touch.

As a writer, she says,
"When pen meets paper, it transforms fleeting thoughts into timeless works of art."

www.ingramcontent.com/pod-product-compliance
Lightning Source LLC
Chambersburg PA
CBHW031646170726
47990CB00019B/2568